HRchitect's Guide to HCM Technology:

What you need to know before your next HCM technology purchase

Jacqueline Kuhn

CONTENTS

FOREWORD

When I took the helm at HRchitect in 2011, we were primarily a recruiting technology implementation firm. Since then, we have grown to support more complex applications, like workforce management and global Human Capital Management (HCM) platforms. However, our Strategic Services practice is what makes HRchitect unique and is a revenue source we are solely in control of.

As the President & CEO, it is up to me to make sure HRchitect is financially sound. Our implementation practices do bring in significant revenues; however, that is tied to the vendors who sell HCM software. Our fate is intrinsically linked to the vendors and, as such, makes us vulnerable.

In contrast, our Strategic Services consulting practice is what makes HRchitect unique and is a revenue source we are solely in control of. This division brings great value to our company, and also provides tremendous value to our clients.

Jacqueline and her team spend their days researching the market, identifying the "next best" thing for HCM technology, and educate our clients, so they make informed decisions. As one of the industry's most sought-after presenters on HCM technology, she has been talking about writing a book like this since joining us in 2012. I am excited that time and resources allowed this to happen.

The content in this book is meant to be educational, but also serves to showcase the incredibly talent we have in our organization. Jacqueline came to HRchitect after spending over 20 years in HR and IT. Her experience running her own successful consulting firm and managing large-scale HCM Technology operations for organizations including Sears, Office Max, and Beam Suntory provides us with the leadership and expertise that our growing consulting practice needs. Julia, Andrew, and Dixie, co-contributors to this book, have been recognized in the company and by our clients for their service excellence. Collectively, they have over 50 years of experience in HR and Technology. This experience, combined with their continuous improvement mindset, ensures our consulting services are of the best quality on the market.

I'm incredibly proud of what our Strategic Services division brings to

HRchitect, and quite frankly, to our industry as a whole. It sets us apart from most other consulting firms in the HCM Technology industry. We provide implementation services *and* strategic services, which I guess you could say makes HRchitect a strategic implementation consulting firm.

On that note, I view all of the consulting service areas that our strategic services team provides as vital to organizations looking to replace or add new HCM Technology. I'm quite frankly puzzled why organizations would ever go it alone. One area that stands out for me, because of the crossover with our implementation services, is Change Management. It's something that is often overlooked, yet crucial to the success of implementing a new system. New technologies and processes can be disruptive to business operations in a positive way. A change management plan is essential to help ensure the acceptance and adoption of new HCM Technology and processes.

At the end of the day, our strategic services practice and philosophy is all about collaboration – collaboration amongst our team and collaboration with our clients from the very first conversation we have about working together. It's a journey that, in many cases, is an ongoing process as environments change, people change, and business needs change. Through it all, our desire is to be of assistance and value to our clients every step of the way of that journey. Our objective from the beginning is to help our clients realize and achieve their organization's goals around HCM Technology by guiding them to a better place than where they are starting from.

It is my hope that the reader comes away with more knowledge than they had when picking up this book, as well as enough knowledge to determine where they need the services of our consultants. Now, more than ever, it is crucial that businesses have the right HCM technology systems in place to allow them to operate efficiently and in the best interests of their employees.

-Matt Lafata, President & CEO of HRchitect

PREFACE

HRchitect is the only consulting firm specializing solely in Human Capital Management (HCM) that delivers expertise around the full lifecycle of HCM technology. We've helped thousands of organizations worldwide of all sizes and industries strategize, select, implement, and support their HCM systems since 1997.

Our team of subject matter experts averages over 15 years in their expertise and work collaboratively to ensure seamless service delivery to our clients. They've also been in your shoes – over 50% of our consulting team comes from an HR practitioner background, allowing them to pair real-world knowledge with consulting expertise – a combination that is hard to find elsewhere.

In our work as consultants, we come across many professionals whose education on Human Capital Management (HCM) technology was provided by their software vendor. While well-intended, we also acknowledge that this education can be biased, as it is typically provided for the purpose of marketing a software product. Our intention with this book is to provide an unbiased overview of the information every HR professional should know about HCM Technology.

The consultants in HRchitect's strategic services consulting practice at the time of this writing collaborated with me on this book, drawing from our collective experience as practitioners and in serving our clients. Our greatest challenge was deciding how much detail should be included. Some topics themselves could be the subject of an entire book! We ultimately agreed that each chapter should provide essential information on the topic that is generally agreed upon in the industry.

Our goal was to create an educational piece that could be read easily and quickly. I hope you find that we accomplished our goal.

- Jacqueline Kuhn, Executive Vice President of Strategic Consulting Services at HRchitect

CHAPTER 1: WHAT IS HCM TECHNOLOGY?

Human Capital Management (HCM) systems are a comprehensive set of software applications used to acquire, manage, develop, and optimize an organization's workforce comprised of employees and non-employee workers.

Initially, HCM systems were built to assist with compliance and to replace manual paper and labor-intensive processes by using the power of computerized processing to create paychecks and generate statutory reports. The legacy applications required a person to be connected to the system at work through desktop computers. Legacy HCM systems were designed for use by Human Resources (HR) professionals, not Managers and Employees.

It is not by accident that HCM systems' evolution aligned with the changing role of the HR professional from data administrator to strategic business partner. HCM technology has changed dramatically since its beginnings in the 1980s. The evolution of technology has made it possible to automate and streamline entire end-to-end organizational HR processes, offering access to more than just the HR Department. In the 1990s, vendors focused on adapting their systems so they could be utilized to deliver information via "self-service" to employees and managers.

In the 2000s, HCM applications were migrated from on-premise servers to the cloud. This enabled all levels of an organization to directly access and interact with HCM applications, anytime, anywhere, and on any device (pc, kiosk, laptop, tablet, and smartphone). This also ushered in a focus on Talent Management, employee engagement, and retention metrics.

- Management use of dashboards, metrics, and analytics to access current, up-to-date information provides valuable and timely data-driven decisions, the ability to make actionable business changes, and the ability to track trends and provide future predictions. Department heads and supervisors also use dashboards and reports to access up-to-date information about their employees, which assists in managing and making decisions about their teams. Managers can initiate, submit, and approve workflow processes through the HCM system. Examples: initiate a salary or job change, submit a promotion request, recommend a candidate for hire, and approve hourly time to be paid.

- Employees access and update their personal information quickly and easily from their pc, tablet, or phone. Examples: access information about benefits and employee handbook, initiate and work with their manager on their performance review, change their family status due to a birth or marriage, and look up remaining vacation time and submit a vacation request online, which is automatically sent to their manager for approval.

Now that the workforce can manage data directly in the HCM system, the HR function has shifted from performing time-consuming administrative tasks to contributing to the company's strategic plan. Through complex reporting and analytics, trends can reveal opportunities or issues in advance. HR can submit and approve workflows submitted by employees or managers. When the workflows are approved, the information is immediately updated in the employee's record. These workflows save time, increase productivity, and reduce costs. For example, a candidate is sent an offer electronically. They sign the offer letter digitally through their phone. Once signed, the system automatically flags them as a new hire and sends them the appropriate information to prepare them for their first day of work.

What are the differences between HRIS (Human Resources Information Systems), HCM (Human Capital Management), and HRMS (Human Resources Management Systems)?

Fundamentally, there are no differences. These are all different names and acronyms that have the same meaning. These terms are used interchangeably by software vendors to market their products. However, the term "HRIS" tends to be viewed as a term referring to the first generation of applications introduced in the 1980s and 1990s.

What capabilities does an HCM System have?

HCM systems are comprised of a Core system and other modules that interface with the Core. Depending on the software vendor, the ability to use pieces of systems capabilities will vary. However, in general, an organization can use all modules or pick and choose which modules they need to implement.

Core Capabilities

The Core HR system is composed of information that is employee-owned as well as company-owned. Employee-owned information includes personal information and preferences, for example, address, bank account information, and willingness to relocate. Company-owned information might include the job, position, pay, and organizational information assigned to the employee.

In a full HCM system, the Core employee record must be established before using other modules. The Core employee record forms the foundational data with the system.

Talent Management Capabilities

While there are applications that stand alone and offer capabilities to support talent management processes, when offered within a full-suite HCM system, an organization benefits from integrated data and true "end-to-end" processes. Whether your organization would benefit from a full-suite HCM system or a standalone solution, these capabilities are standard in what is considered Talent Management applications.

Talent Acquisition

The processes for acquiring talent including sourcing candidates, intake of applications and resumes, assessment of candidates, interviewing, extending offers, and any background and reference checking processes. Applications supporting these processes are commonly called Applicant Tracking Systems (ATS) and Candidate Relationship Management Systems (CRM).

Onboarding

The processes for bringing new employees into the organization. Onboarding includes any paperwork needed for legal/compliance purposes, collecting new hire information, enrolling in benefits, and taking any required new hire training. Another key piece of Onboarding is the process of assimilating the person to the company. This might include setting expectations for the first 30/60/90 days and can also include activities for the hiring manager or mentor to complete.

Performance Achievement

This includes the processes that assess skills, competencies, and achievement of set goals and objectives. This also includes creating Development Plans for the achievement of performance objectives. Although this is often called Performance "Management," we call this "Achievement" instead, as the intent of the systems supporting these processes are for employees to succeed in their goals and achieve their career goals.

Succession Planning

This encompasses the processes for assessing the achievement potential for individuals commonly called "High Potential" and "Readiness," and metrics that help to understand the consequences of turnover like "Risk of Loss" and "Impact of Loss." These metrics are used by leaders to identify position replacements, "Successors." The key to succession planning applications is the ability to identify key positions in the organization. Then based on the requirements of the position, the succession planning application will automatically suggest individuals within the organization that can fill the position. The metrics are used to understand the impact on the individual and the organization if they become a successor. A grid, or "9 box," is commonly used as a tool within the application to analyze this data.

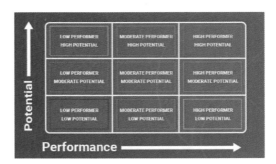

Learning / Training

Known in the HCM technology world as a Learning Management System (LMS), this refers to the ability to offer and track learning activities and experiences. The LMS provides the learner the ability to watch training videos, enroll in traditional classroom training, store and track training activities in a "transcript," and access resource information provided by the company in the form of documents.

Compensation Management

This capability refers to the processes for the management of compensation plans and processes. The Core HR system stores a person's components of pay that go into the paycheck. The Compensation Management application provides tools for allocating compensation increases, conducting equity analysis, planning and modeling the focal processes of merit and bonus, tracking employee rewards, and incorporating benchmark data like target market rates. This module does rely on the data in Core, as that is where the person's Job, Location, and Years of Experience reside; thus, integration between Core and the Compensation module is key.

Recognition

Where the compensation system provides the monetary reward for achievement, the recognition system provides the feedback mechanisms. It empowers teams throughout the organization to recognize one another for the great work they do every day and to recognize significant achievements and milestones. Common characteristics of recognition systems are the ability to provide feedback in a public social feed, awarding of digital badges, and a direct tie into rewards that can be earned.

Time, Attendance, and Workforce Management

This application is perhaps the one most often NOT owned by HR and very often is independent of the HCM Suite. In manufacturing, healthcare and other high hourly labor industries, this is often owned by the Operations group. These applications are often complemented with a time clock device that allows a person to "punch" in and out of work. However, these devices are often not a part of the HCM Suite, and are purchased separately. The capabilities of these applications include:

- Managing time worked by having employees punch in and out and applying rules to the time worked based on the work schedule and applicable local and federal law.
- Managing time off by creating rules that determine how much time off a person is entitled to, tracking how much has been taken, and automating the request for time off process.

- Introducing labor efficiencies by automatically creating work schedules based on employee skills, availability, and the amount of labor needed per shift.
- Budgeting by incorporating pay information when looking at labor patterns and forecasting the need for labor in the future and the projected labor cost.

Technologies that enable processes and decision making

- **Workflows:** Wrapped around Core and the other modules and include routing, approvals, and notifications. Workflows can be initiated by employees, managers, or HR. Workflows can also be triggered by a change to the data.
- **Business Intelligence and Reporting:** Features include regulatory and compliance reports, organizational reports, analytics, metrics, and dashboards. Many HCM systems are delivered with a standard set of reports that can be copied and modified to meet the organization's needs. Additional "ad hoc" reporting tools may also be offered to create reports and dashboards from scratch.
- **Interfaces:** These are both to and from other systems. Interfaces are used to connect and share information to and from external systems and vendors, such as general ledger and benefit providers.
- **Security:** Provided to allow each organization to identify an individual's access into the system. Security is set up based on "role," and one's role in the organization can determine their access level. These levels are defined by "what" and "who."
    - "What" pieces of data within the application is a person granted access to, and what can they do within the system? Can they change the information or just view it?
    - "Who" in the organization does the person have access to?
- **Artificial Intelligence (AI) tools**
    - **Sentiment analysis:** Analysis of text to identify the "meaning" behind the words. For example, take the text

of a performance review and identify if the meaning is positive, negative, or neutral.

o **Chatbots:** Computer programs that simulate interactive human conversation.

o **Robotic process automation (RPA):** Software/robot that emulates human execution of tasks via existing user interfaces.

o **Machine learning:** A type of AI that provides computers with the ability to learn without being explicitly programmed.

o **Predictive analytics:** The practice of extracting information from existing data sets to determine patterns and predict possible future outcomes and trends.

CHAPTER 2: HR SERVICE DELIVERY

What is HR Service Delivery?

On any given day, employees are looking for answers to questions and information about everything from career opportunities, time off policies, paychecks, benefits, and more. The people, processes and technology used to answer those questions make up the HR Service Delivery model.

This model forms the foundation of the HR Technology Strategy and requirements for the subsequent HR application purchase.

To create a Service Delivery model to support the business needs and people strategies, an organization needs to identify what services will be delivered and how they will be delivered. For services that will be delivered in person, organizations also need to identify who will be responsible for providing that service.

What processes should be included in the HR Service Delivery Strategy?

All processes that are owned by the HR function should be included in the HR Service Delivery Strategy. All processes that touch employees that are not owned by the HR function but require information from an HR System to be carried out should also be included in the HR Service Delivery Strategy. The processes need to be thought of in terms of the employee life cycle from sourcing a potential candidate to exiting that person. Common processes are Talent Acquisition, Onboarding, Benefits Enrollment, Performance Reviews, and Learning & Development. Some processes that are not necessarily owned by HR but need to be discussed as part of the lifecycle are Payroll, Time and Attendance, and expense reimbursement. The below list includes all processes that are typically considered in the HR Service Delivery Strategy:

- Recruiting
- Pre-Hire Onboarding
- Assimilation / Integration of New Hires / Joiners
- Benefits Enrollment
- Employee Personal Information Changes

- Employee Job and Pay Changes
- Payroll Related Processes
- Time and Absence
- Performance Achievement and Development
- Learning / Training
- Compensation Processes
- Talent Review
- Succession Planning
- Workforce Planning
- Expense Management
- Relocation
- Off-Boarding / Processing Leavers

How are the processes/services delivered?

Once the processes are identified, you need to determine how each of the processes will be "served up." Which processes will be transactional, and which are informational only?

A transactional process is one where a person must provide information and execute a process. A Change of Address is an example of a transactional process. An Informational process is one where a person seeks information or understanding. Reviewing the time off policy is an example of an informational process.

When designing **transactional processes**, consider which processes will be executed by employees or managers using an application and which are going to be executed for them. For each process, there are many decisions to be made, and the following questions are those that are key:

- Will the process be delivered via an application as a first action?
    - Does this process need to be available to non-employee persons?
    - Will this be for all people or certain types of employees?
    - What languages does the application need to support for the process?
    - What hours does the application need to be available to support this process?
    - Will access to an application be granted via a mobile device?
        - At work?
        - Outside of work?
        - Does the application need to restrict certain types of employee groups during non-working

hours (e.g., hourly employees)?
- Will the process require an approval step? If so, how will the approval be carried out within the application?
- When will a person be engaged in this process?

For **informational processes**, it is a best practice to deliver these processes via HCM systems. A person should only be engaged to support the process if there is an exception situation. To enable the best user experience, the best practice is to personalize the application. When the employee user accesses information, the application should only present to the employee information that is relevant to them. For example, if the employee is looking for the holiday calendar for their location, they should not be presented with all of the company holiday calendars globally. Therefore, the first consideration points are what information will be accessed via the application, how the information will be stored and indexed/tagged and provided, and where the documents will be stored. For each informational process, there are many decisions to be made. The following questions are key to helping with that decision making:

- What are the requirements for the personalization of this process? Department, Location, Employee Type, Languages?
- Do we have the content/data to support a personalized experience for this process?
- What hours does the application need to be available to support this process?
- Will access to an application be granted via a mobile device?
  - At work?
  - Outside of work?
  - Does the application need to restrict certain types of employees during non-working hours (e.g., hourly employees)?
- When will a person be engaged in this process?

Who performs various activities for each process/service?

Perhaps the most important part of the HR Service Delivery Model is the plan for when and how a person is engaged in a process. The point at which an employee needs assistance is usually when the online applications are not providing them the information they are looking for, or a transaction is not working as expected. The availability and knowledge of the person designated to help in a specific situation will make a difference in the user experience. Not only do you need to identify who will engage, but you also need to determine if the location of the people who will engage will be centralized, regionalized, or completely decentralized.

A centralized model implies that all persons that support the processes will be co-located in one physical area. Thus the hours of operation and ability for people to support the business will be key. For example, if support is needed from 7 am to 7 pm Eastern Time, staffing a service center in the Pacific Time Zone during the morning hours might be a challenge.

When regionalized, centers are located in different parts of the world to serve the organization better. Often in a global organization, there will be a service center in the U.S., one in Europe, and one in Asia, so those regions have coverage.

The decentralized model is one where the people supporting HR processes are located anywhere in the world. Having the right service center technology is especially key for this model to be successful.

The **applications** that support service delivery are an extension of the HR Team. These applications must be easy to use and access, support all languages native to your employees and be maintained so information and data remain current and relevant.

Along with Core HCM applications, there are complementary applications designed to enhance service delivery. These systems have functionality such as the ability to log requests, a chat function, FAQ's, and a knowledge base.

The ability to log requests and the ability to route those requests to the appropriate persons should be a prioritized requirement. In this way, you can be sure that questions are answered in a logical and efficient manner.

The chat function is helpful when a person needs basic help in finding information that does not necessarily require logging a ticket. For example, you may find it useful during benefit enrollment to have a chat function to quickly get an answer to an employee plan question. That would allow you to reserve the opening of a formal ticket to when that question results in a potential policy exception that needs further review and approval.

The FAQ's and Knowledge Base are complementary tools. A Knowledge Base is a collection of informational documents about policy, processes, and potentially forms used to request services. The FAQ's allow for a quick answer without having to search the knowledge base. The key to the success of the FAQ function is the word "frequently." Maintaining a library of questions and answers is time-consuming. That library must be updated whenever the answer may change. Having a set of FAQ's that are outdated will raise questions of the validity of the tools and generate more ticket and phone requests. Thus, the organization must determine which questions will be answered within the FAQ section and which will not. Remember that when establishing the FAQ library, if a question is asked for which there is no answer established, you need to direct the person to a resource that can answer their question. It's critical not to abandon the inquiry.

A cohesive HR Service Delivery Model and Strategy will enable your organization to develop a comprehensive HCM Technology Strategy. The HCM Technology Strategy enables the purchases of the right technology system, making for successful implementations and results in employees having a great user experience, which drives engagement.

Your HCM Technology journey starts here, with HR Service Delivery.

CHAPTER 3: THE HCM TECHNOLOGY STRATEGY

Taking a journey without a plan is never advised. Without a roadmap of where you are going, how you are getting there, and when you anticipate arriving, it's next to impossible to keep your journey on track. The HCM Technology Strategy is the plan for your journey in developing the processes and applications that support the HR Service Delivery Model. Having an HCM Technology Strategy is important as it becomes the foundation for the evaluation, selection, and implementation of these solutions. Without one, systems are purchased based on "in the moment" needs, without taking into consideration the bigger picture. Other benefits of having a strategy include:

- Ensuring applications are properly integrated for a better end-to-end user experience
- Maximizing the investment in applications with increased ROI
- A "single source of the truth" for information, or as close as possible, for consistent data used for decision making
- Adoption by, and alignment with, the business

Five activities need to be performed in order to create an HCM Technology Strategy:

1. Create a set of objectives for the future state.
2. Perform a review of each people process.
3. Create the strategy for the future state.
4. Create the business case for the future state.
5. Create the Strategy Management Plan.

Create the objectives

When creating the objectives, you should think about how the new applications will support the business and HR strategies and processes, along with supporting the desired HR Service Delivery Model. In thinking of objectives, think about what the experience would look like for the various stakeholders if the new solution would be fully implemented. Think about Managers, Leaders, HR Business Partners, Contractors, and third-party vendors. The objective should have a "who," "what," and "how." Who are the people this applies to? What are they going to be doing in the future? How will they do the activity? Some examples of objectives are:

- Our HR Business Partners can easily review requisitions on a mobile device
- Employees can request time off on a mobile device
- Reporting that is reliable and consumable as information is pushed out to leaders who will view it on their tablets

Perform a review of each "people process"

We refer to them as "People Processes" as while most are owned by the HR function, some may not be, such as Time and Attendance, which is often owned by Operations. However, to create a strategy and achieve end-to-end processes, all of them must be included, and they are:

- Talent Acquisition
- Onboarding
- Employee Records Management
- Benefits Administration
- Payroll
- Time & Absence Tracking
- Compensation Management
- Performance Achievement
- Development and Learning
- Talent and Succession Planning
- Workforce Planning

This review needs to include the processes themselves, the applications supporting these processes, and any interdependencies. Based on the information gathered, you will identify areas where current HCM systems are not supporting key processes, manual processes that can be automated, and areas where standardization or single process ownership are required.

In parallel to the inventory exercise, conduct interviews with key users of the systems to obtain their feedback on the current state process, and gather needs for the future state.

As a result of these interviews, you will be able to determine which systems and processes are underperforming and where they may conflict with company goals and critical business operations. This should also result in an understanding of the prioritization of processes.

Create the strategy

Taking the information gathered, create the HCM Technology Strategy to fit the HR Service Delivery Model. You will look at the information from the interviews to understand the critical business needs and your current system and process inventory, assessing their ability to meet your critical business needs. This will help you determine what to keep, cut, and create to support your most critical business needs. The strategy components should include the current state, strategy options, and recommendations.

Current State: This includes the statements about the key issues and challenges in the current state that are addressed by the strategy. Specific applications and processes are to be identified along with their impact on the support of business operations. Take care not to focus too much on the impact on the HR function itself, as the strategy should support the processes, which in turn support business needs. For example, a recruiting process challenge for a recruiter is not as impactful as the challenge of getting a new employee hired quickly. Keep in mind, if your current state looks too much like HR complaining about how difficult it is to do their job, this can and will jeopardize the likelihood of your strategy getting approved.

Strategy Options: The technology options in the marketplace today are vast, and because of this, there will be more than one strategy that is viable. The goal is to determine which approach makes the most sense for your organization. The best practice is to create a minimum of three options. This will usually be complete enough to vet the best possible scenarios. When building your options, include information about the full solution, the benefits to be gained, and the challenges that may be encountered. Each option should also have an estimated cost, including implementation fees, annual fees, and any resources that would need to be hired or re-skilled in order to support the applications in the strategy. Lastly, the options should have a timeline of when they would be executed. The timeline should reflect calendar quarters as there would not be enough information to get into specific weeks and months at this time. Remember, what you present in your strategy is what you will be held to accomplish, so keep it realistic!

Recommendations: In presenting the strategy to leadership, you will need to make a recommendation. While you need to be prepared to defend your recommendation, if you have clearly stated your objectives and options, the recommendation should not be a surprise. To help you in determining if your recommendation stands up to scrutiny, vet your strategy with key stakeholders in the organization before presenting it to leadership. Not only will this give you practice in presenting your strategy, but it will also give you allies for your strategy. If you can say that the recommendation has been reviewed and agreed upon as the best strategy by other stakeholders, you will increase the likelihood of getting it approved.

Business Case

A business case will help to obtain approval for your technology strategy. The HRchitect Business Case Framework is based on a three-pillar approach of Productivity, Risk, and Cost.

Productivity: Quantifies the time spent on activities today and uses benchmark data to identify time savings that can be achieved with new technology. Based on the strategy process inventory, assess the time it takes to complete the activities within the process itself as well as to maintain the applications that support the process. Make sure you include time spent on workarounds or manual events. Based on your strategy, you will determine if time will be saved in certain areas by the use of better tools and automation or if time will increase in areas that you are not investing time in today.

The resulting time spent will be your productivity number. If the number is a savings, you will want to identify how these hours saved will be translated into organizational changes. They could be a reduction in headcount, reallocating headcount, or avoidance of new hires as the people affected can take on more work activities. In the unlikely event that your productivity number increases, you will need to identify how this will better serve the business in providing valuable capabilities and services.

Risk: Identifies the risks in the current environment that can be mitigated with new technology. These risks include those involving the use of old, outdated software, the limitations of those systems, and processes that are a compliance risk due to the use of those systems. Other risks to consider are security and global data privacy/security.

Depending on the system you are looking to replace and the vendor provider, there may be additional risks that the vendor may no longer be viable, thus risks to your business continuity. If your current applications experience significant periods of downtime or encounter many errors, these also are risks to business continuity.

For the future state, you will want to state how a newer software vendor provides a secure application. Obtaining service and support information from the vendor along with statements about compliance will help to build the case that the newer application can mitigate the current risk.

Cost: Identifies the people and technology costs involved in operating the systems today and those required in the future to quantify the savings or investment opportunities. This aspect of the business case needs to include real budget savings or investments, also called "hard dollar" amounts, as compared to the productivity and risk components that are commonly called "soft dollar" amounts.

This is where your actual costs associated with maintaining your current systems are reflected. You will need to include hardware, software, people resources, consultants, and any other fees related to running the applications today. If you have in-house applications, any depreciation of the hardware or software is included in these numbers (if you are unsure how to obtain this, partner with your Finance organization).

For the future state strategy, you will need to include the costs to procure and implement the new applications as well as ongoing needs for resources to support the applications purchased.

The difference between the current and future state will be your "hard dollar" savings or investment amount.

Once you have the Productivity, Risk, and Costs identified, create an executive-level presentation that tells the story of the overall business case for your strategy. If you are not experienced in doing this, hiring a consulting firm like HRchitect to assist will help to ensure your strategy is approved.

The Strategy Management Plan

Having invested time, money, and resources to develop the HCM Strategy, properly executing it will require a Management Plan. Otherwise, the chances of the strategy becoming "shelf-ware" increase. Simply put, a Management Plan is a structure by which strategy adherence is monitored, and the strategy itself adjusted to reflect business and market changes.

Establish an HCM and Technology Management Team composed of your organization's HR, IT, and key business stakeholders. The goal of this team is to balance ongoing operational priorities against the initiatives of the strategy in order to make progress on the strategy while continuing important projects on the existing platforms. This team should also meet regularly (quarterly at a minimum) to review the HCM and technology strategy and adjust timelines and/or shift resources based on changing business needs or market conditions.

The outcomes of the strategy management meetings will make sure that ongoing operations are addressed while keeping the strategy moving forward.

CHAPTER 4: SYSTEM EVALUATION & SELECTION

When selecting a new HCM system, there are six key areas of activity to ensure the evaluation project results in a sound investment:

1. Objectives and decision drivers
2. Business requirements
3. Request for Proposal (RFP)
4. Vendor demonstrations
5. Vendor evaluation
6. Contract negotiations

Objectives and Decision Drivers

The initial step of the evaluation project is to define and confirm the project scope, objectives, and timeline. This is also the time to identify decision drivers, which are the overarching criteria on which a solution will be selected. These drivers go beyond simply evaluating based on features and functions and provide a fact-based, objective, and systematic method for a technology selection. Identifying these criteria will allow the selection team to make an informed decision, which will lead to a better product fit, increased user buy-in, and greater ROI.

When establishing decision drivers, determine which will be used and the priority each will be assigned. Start by identifying any which are not important to the organization and can be eliminated. Next, determine which drivers are most important, and if not met, would eliminate a vendor from consideration. Last, rank the decision drivers in order of importance.

The best practice decision drivers for evaluating HCM Technology are:

- **Configurability by HR:** The degree to which the system can be modified with no vendor or internal IT support using standard system administration and configuration tools.

- **Cost and ROI:** The ability to achieve the desired return on investment and to fit within the budget set for HR software. This includes not only implementation and annual software fees but also the cost to maintain it, including training, third-party, and ongoing support costs.
- **Ease of Integration:** The ability to and complexity of integrating the vendor's product with existing applications, systems, or third parties that may need to share data.
- **Functionality:** The degree to which the product meets the important and unique functional business requirements with standard functionality.
- **Global Capabilities:** The ability of the product to provide multi-language capabilities, support multiple currencies, and support country-specific regulations and data privacy laws.
- **Operational Effectiveness:** The product's ability to streamline the company's processes and make the organization more effective.
- **Scalability:** The software's ability to scale up or down when the company needs change due to growth or reductions in employees, locations, or other relevant volumes.
- **Services and Support:** The services the vendor offers, the level of support they provide both during and after implementation and during system upgrades, and the skills and bench strength of the support team.
- **Technology:** The vendor's ability to provide a safe, secure, and reliable system; also considers the internet browsers and mobile devices supported as well as the frequency of software updates.
- **Usability:** The perception of ease of use of the system, including look and feel and intuitiveness of the user interface. While this is the most subjective of the decision drivers and cannot be assessed until a vendor demo, it is very important as it impacts user adoption and the degree of training and support required.
- **Vendor Viability:** Considers the vendor company as a whole, including financial strength, length of time in business, the maturity of the product, R&D investment, product roadmap, client base by numbers and industry, client retention, and recent new sales.

Business Requirements

In order to select a system that will work for your organization, a clearly defined requirements document is crucial. There are two main components of requirements that need to be documented - functional and technical requirements.

Functional requirements support the business processes and objectives. Work with HR process owners, subject matter experts, end-users, and management to understand gaps and challenges in the current environment and processes. Look for opportunities to standardize and create more efficient processes where possible. It is important that the functional requirements reflect future state business processes. If you carry forward requirements based on current processes, you will also carry forward the current challenges associated with those processes into a new system. In order to gain efficiency and optimize the use of technology, requirements should be defined based on the desired future state.

When documenting functional requirements, include enough detail to give prospective vendors enough information to understand the process, function, and related data the system needs to support and why it is important or how it ties into your business objectives. Avoid trying to prescribe specific steps on *how* the system should support the requirement and allow vendors to recommend how their solution can best support your need.

For example, suppose Compensation is in scope, and you have a very complex bonus calculation process that considers the employee's job level, sales performance, and the company's overall performance. In that case, your requirement should not dictate the process and exact steps to be taken. It should, however, provide details for the vendor on how each factor impacts the bonus, where or how those factors are defined, the calculation formula, and other details about the result needed. Then ask the vendor to show you how this could be done in their system.

Technical requirements in the RFP for HCM cloud-based applications will collect information on the technical aspects of the vendor's application. Keep in mind that in a cloud-based world, you cannot dictate how the application is technically built, so you need to focus on whether the technical components are a fit for your organizational requirements. Thus, the technical requirements must include an understanding of the vendor's architecture, hosting, data security, authentication options, certifications, business continuity plans, service level agreements, as well as the ability to support integrations with other internal company systems or third parties that may be needed. Obtain copies of the vendor's backup and recovery procedures to understand how your organization may be impacted in the event of a disaster. Include details on any known systems which may remain in place that will need to pass data to or obtain data from the new HCM.

Once documented, these requirements will be used to develop a Request for Proposal (RFP), vendor demonstration script, and to serve as a guide to evaluate potential vendor products.

Request for Proposal (RFP)

The RFP process involves two activities - determining which vendors will be invited to respond and creating the actual RFP document, which will be distributed to those vendors.

A typical RFP timeline is between ten and twelve weeks. HRchitect has developed a unique **Fast Path RFP** process, which trims the process down to six to eight weeks. Some of the differences are highlighted below.

Based on the scope and complexity of functionality required and the decision drivers that have been established, identify a shortlist of vendors who should receive the RFP. If using an experienced consulting firm like HRchitect, we will be able to recommend vendors best suited to your organization's needs. Otherwise, additional research will be needed for you to create your vendor list.

The RFP is designed to get specific answers from the vendor as to how they meet detailed requirements. It contains information about your organization and information requested of the vendor.

The information about your organization that you should include in the RFP is:

- **Company Information:** This should include company size, location(s), number and types of employees (e.g., full-time, part-time, salary, hourly). Include information about your company's core business and any special considerations the vendor may need to know, such as upcoming expansion, merger, acquisition, or growth. Details about the project scope, project objectives, and timeline should also be provided. This will help the vendor determine if they are a good fit.

- **Functional Business Requirements:** The list of your requirements must be prioritized to indicate which requirements are most critical. The lack of ability to support these requirements would likely cause a vendor to be eliminated and should be marked as top priorities. Next, indicate those requirements which are desired or "nice to have" functionality. Then there are those requirements that fall into the category of functionality that you anticipate will be needed in the future but may not be utilized right away. By clearly defining the priority of your requirements, vendors can focus on those that are most critical. This prioritization is also used when evaluating vendor proposals.

- **Technical Requirements:** Your detailed technical requirements should include a list of known integrations with other systems or third parties that must be supported.
- **Evaluation Timeline:** Information on when vendor questions should be submitted, a deadline by which vendors must confirm their intention to bid, due date for RFP responses, timing for when demonstrations will occur, and when final vendor selection is expected to occur should be included.

Information requested of the vendor in the RFP:

- **Vendor Information:** Request information about the vendor company that will help determine how they stack up against established decision drivers. Details about company size, revenue, number and tenure of employees, and number of implementations of similar size and scope to your organization should be requested to help gauge vendor viability.
- **Functional Business Requirements:** The vendor should respond to your functional business requirements to confirm if each of your requirements can be met. You should also ask vendors to indicate whether any of your requirements will require an additional module(s) to be purchased and/or third-party functionality to fully support the business need. In a standard RFP approach, the vendor is expected to provide a written description of how they meet each requirement. In HRchitect's Fast Path approach, vendors are only required to provide an explanation for any requirements they cannot fully meet. They will have the opportunity to show how they meet requirements as part of the demonstration phase.
- **Technical Requirements:** From a technical perspective, ask the vendor to provide information about their hosting, security model, business continuity plan, and support and maintenance of their software, including frequency of and process for updates. If detailed technical requirements were identified for your organization, the vendor should respond to their ability to support those as well.
- **Service Level Agreements (SLAs):** Request information about the vendor's SLAs. This should indicate what levels of service can be expected for support of the software, expected availability of the product, support hours, escalation procedures, and maintenance windows.
- **Cost Proposal:** Ask for a detailed cost breakout based on all functionality in scope and implementation plan. The cost proposal should include licensing fees, implementation costs, any other one-

time fees, training costs, rate sheets, and other costs that may apply. If a phased implementation is expected, it is important to understand how and when costs are incurred as well as when the licensing fees begin.

Once your vendor list has been created and the RFP document finalized, the RFP should be distributed to the vendors.

Upon receipt, each vendor's response and proposal should be reviewed to identify any gaps, concerns, and follow up questions needed to continue the evaluation. In the standard approach, you review and evaluate all responses to determine which vendors will be invited to demonstrate their product. We recommend this shortlist of vendors be limited to your top three to four choices. With HRchitect's Fast Path RFP process, all vendors submitting responses are invited to demonstrate as they have already been vetted to ensure they meet 80% or greater of our client's functional requirements.

Vendor Demonstrations

The purpose of vendor demonstrations is to provide another data point for decision making. The RFP written response indicates whether the vendor can perform the functionality needed. The demonstration is the opportunity to see how the system supports that functionality and provides the ability to evaluate vendors against the "Usability" decision driver.

Demonstrations need to reflect how the software will work for your organization, given your company's processes and data. The best way to achieve this is through a scripted demonstration. The script should focus on processes in scope and direct the vendor to show how they meet your top priority functional business requirements.

It is important that the correct audience attends the demonstrations. All key stakeholders and process owners should be invited. While they may not be able to evaluate every functional area, it is vital that they attend and evaluate the area(s) most relevant to them. By having each stakeholder attend the relevant topics for every demo, they will see what each vendor has to offer and how each would support the business requirements. This increases the probability of selecting the best solution for the organization and helps obtain buy-in and acceptance of the new system.

At the conclusion of each demonstration, while the details are still fresh, evaluate how closely the vendor met the requirements from the script across each process area. It is best practice to provide a scoring matrix to all demonstration attendees for ease of collecting input on vendor demonstration performance. The matrix may include weighting and priorities, along with the scoring methodology.

Vendor Evaluation & Due Diligence

Follow-up conversations or more in-depth demos of critical areas may be necessary to understand the vendor's ability to support your needs more clearly. Reference calls should be conducted with your top choices to obtain further insight. This detail, combined with demonstration scores, should be reviewed and an evaluation matrix assembled.

To avoid purely emotional or subjective reasoning in decision making, the evaluation matrix should incorporate your prioritized decision drivers and each vendor's performance against those as well as your business requirements. These should be weighted accordingly to ensure the highest priority decision drivers and "must-have" business requirements provide the greatest influence on each vendor's overall scoring.

If scoring is so close that there is no clear leader, be prepared to analyze the vendor scores further. Look for factors that truly differentiate one vendor from the other based on your highest priority decision drivers and business requirements. For example, Vendor A and Vendor B scored the same in functionality and usability based on the demonstration. However, after due diligence and reference calls, concerns were raised about the lack of or timeliness of ongoing support from Vendor B as well as a pattern of issues following their system updates. If Services and Support is a top decision driver, this would tip the scales in Vendor A's favor.

Contract Negotiation

This step in the process is critical to assure that the product selected, based on the information in the RFP and what was demonstrated by the vendor, is, in fact, the product that will be delivered.

You may wish to begin contract discussions with your top two vendors while you continue to analyze and evaluate them. Contract terms and conditions vary, and many are non-negotiable. Having two vendors in play at this point of the process allows you to continue with your evaluation while also providing an opportunity to identify potential deal-breakers that may arise during negotiations. By keeping two vendors in play, you maintain momentum as you work towards a final decision.

Contracting for cloud software is unique. If you have not negotiated this type of contract before, a consulting firm like HRchitect can provide feedback and offer suggestions about contract terms and conditions to help you negotiate the best contract possible.

CHAPTER 5: IMPLEMENTATION OF HCM SYSTEMS

What to Expect

After selecting and contracting with a new vendor(s) for an HCM Application, the next phase of the journey is beginning to plan for implementation.

Implementing a new HCM system should be considered a tremendous opportunity for change. It is your organization's opportunity to improve upon and streamline operations, create a better employee experience, and enhance your HR Service Delivery Model. The implementation will require a great deal of planning and diligence throughout the project. The opportunity for positive change will not come without a lot of hard work and dedication. Expect and plan for resources being over-allocated at certain points throughout the project. There will be challenges with scheduling resources, and it is important to recognize this when building project plans. It is important to build buffers into plans wherever possible to avoid bottlenecks that result from a lack of resources. A good plan and execution can mitigate the risk of burning out resources and ensure a successful project. Project managers and executive sponsors should be checking in regularly throughout the project to understand where resources may be overallocated and step in to provide relief when needed. Burnout can be a challenge, but with proper management, it can be avoided.

HCM technology implementations are about more than getting access to a new system and converting data. There are many moving parts to be considered when planning to implement new systems. The following are some of the most critical considerations and risks to implementation projects and suggestions for mitigation.

- Is Payroll in scope? If so, when do you plan to transition? If Payroll is in scope, a January 1 go-live is ideal as you will be able to avoid converting opening balances, which can be a labor-intensive and time-consuming process. Converting on January 1, you will process W-2s through your old payroll vendor and start fresh on January 1 with the new Vendor. This helps mitigate the risk of W-2 issues for employees and saves the implementation team a lot of time since you won't have to convert opening balances.

  The drawback to converting on January 1 is that it places a lot of pressure on project teams to prepare for year-end on the legacy system while having to train and test with the new vendor. This can make for an extraordinarily busy and hectic year-end process, so it is something to consider when deciding if January 1 is the date you want to convert.

- A second alternative is converting at the start of a calendar quarter. When you convert at the beginning of a quarter, it will require converting opening balances from the legacy system to new providers, which will include an additional effort to convert and validate. By converting at the start of a quarter, you will have a clean break from a tax reporting standpoint. Your legacy provider will report a full quarter of taxable wages just before you close out with them. Your new vendor will then report out for all wages after going live.

- It is best to avoid mid-quarter go-lives, but if that is the only option, then it will be required that you convert Year to Date and Quarter to Date opening balances. This will increase efforts to convert and validate the data against legacy systems.

- Benefits Open Enrollment Dates are another area to consider if you are looking at a benefits solution as part of your implementation. Will you perform Open Enrollment in your existing system or new systems? What benefit data needs to be converted based on this decision?

- When do your licenses expire with legacy systems? Is there a realistic opportunity to renew for a shorter period as a contingency plan? It is important to realistically estimate and plan your implementation timeframe to allow enough time for implementation comfortably before your existing licenses expire. If there is any doubt around timing, it is important to have a contingency plan where you can continue to use a legacy HCM/Payroll provider and avoid any disruption to employees being paid while having a functioning HCM system if a go-live date can't be achieved.

- What does your overall system landscape look like? What are the critical integrations that need to be established prior to go-live on a new HCM system?

- How much of your data are you planning to convert from your legacy system? You should make this decision based on how critical it is to regularly access the data and how difficult it is to retain access once you have sunset the legacy system. Most cloud HCM solutions will give you the option to convert between 3-7 years of data such as job history and employment history into your new HCM system. If data is clean and easy to map to new systems, this is a worthwhile exercise. You may also wish to convert data from a legacy provider into another type of data warehouse if IT functions will facilitate it. The driving factor behind these decisions should be to retain access to critical data while minimizing the technical effort to convert.

- Resource allocations and reliance on other systems should also be monitored throughout the project. Are there any other large enterprise projects ongoing that could have a negative impact on resources like IT/HR or business leaders involved in testing? What ancillary systems do you have that rely on the timing of implementing a new HCM system or vice versa? Are any of these systems being sunset or upgraded in conjunction with your HCM project?

Resources Needed

There are a number of critical resources required to staff the implementation of a new HCM system. The most common on any project are outlined below:

Subject Matter Experts (SMEs): These are the people who have deep functional expertise about the processes and requirements for the areas which are being implemented. More than likely, the subject matter experts were the key stakeholders that were interviewed when gathering business requirements. Typically, they are the HR Business Partners, Payroll

Processors, Compensation Analyst, HRIS, Benefits Analyst, and similar types of jobholders. They are responsible for creating the functional business requirements and specifications for the system configurations and reports. SMEs will also be heavily involved during the data conversion and testing phases of the project.

Functional and Technical Product Experts: These are the people who have deep functional and technical knowledge of the product being implemented. These people know how the product works from a process perspective, understand some of the nuances to make specific features work, and have product configuration expertise. With SaaS HCM implementations, these resources are provided by the vendor or from a 3rd party partner like HRchitect. These resources will guide and educate your internal teams through all phases of the implementation.

These resources may also be called **System Consultant/Implementation Consultant** who are resources provided by the vendor or a 3rd party like HRchitect. When used, they will remain on the project team throughout the design and build, assist with the testing process, and typically serve as the main point of contact for system questions, configuration assistance, and support through all phases of testing.

Other Technical Experts: When implementing an HR system, there are other technical components that need resources, whether they are internal or from another 3rd party vendor that will integrate with your new HR system. While most of these resources do not need to be dedicated full time to the project, they need to be available at critical points to keep the implementation on track. These resources can include IT security, benefit vendor developers and analysts, internal analytics teams, or other technical resources that will need to access and interpret data from your HCM system.

Project Managers: A successful implementation of a new HR System will require a project manager to ensure that the project stays on track from a budget and timing perspective. Large enterprise projects can be very complex, so it is critical to have a dedicated resource on the vendor side and on your team to build and manage project plans. There are a variety of tools and resources used to manage these projects, but regardless of the tool, the role of the PM is to hold everyone accountable, stay on target with dates, and manage any escalations that come up throughout the project.

Executive Sponsor: A strong executive sponsor who is actively involved in the process can make a project run much smoother. A strong leader on your team will help keep resources engaged and motivated. They can assist with removing barriers to success and help drive critical decisions throughout the project. The most successful projects have a strong leadership presence that is actively involved, motivates, and empowers the team to drive success. The Sponsor will also be responsible for resolving issues and driving decisions that need executive-level approval.

Typical Implementation Phases

Software implementations may have slight variations in phase names and implementation methodology depending on which vendor or consulting firm you are using. Still, the general principles are the same whether you are looking at implementing Core HR and payroll, a talent suite, or a 3rd party benefits provider. All technology implementations will go through the following stages: *Plan, Design and Build/Configuration, Test, Go Live, and Support.*

Plan

The planning stage is where you transition from the sales cycle over to the implementation process. On the vendor side, the sales team will share information obtained during the sales cycle with the implementation project team. This will include contact information, project scope, general company structure, and any other relevant information to help the implementation team get acclimated to the project.

During the early stages of the planning phase, your organization should be focused on the following:

- Identifying project team members.
- Aligning with Executive leadership/sponsorship. It is important that the leader be present through planning and kick-off to get the team engaged and motivated and address upfront concerns.
- Determining go-live dates for each technology/module that will be implemented.
- Notifying existing vendors of your intent to leave and starting transition plans.
  - Process flows and documentation:
    - It is important to have a solid understanding of all your current HR business workflows and approval requirements to modify and build-out in the new system.

  - Policy and Procedure documentation:
    - Being prepared with policy documents like PTO plans, leave policies, and benefit programs will make the design phase move more efficiently.

  - Required Integrations:
    - Integrations will be a critical part of the project that can take significant time to build and test. The

more work you can do upfront to understand the required integrations and document these requirements with vendors, the quicker the build process can start. In turn, this will help ensure all integrations are ready for go-live.

o   Project Team Training needs to be planned. While end-user training is usually a component of the Change Management Plan, the key project team members need to be trained on the application so they can be educated contributors to the implementation.

The last critical component of the planning phase is the project kickoff meeting that introduces the project to all the team members from the vendor/consultant side and your internal project team. This kickoff meeting will also be an opportunity for the two teams to get acquainted with each other and start to develop rapport.

After the kickoff, detailed project plans will be created. This will involve project managers from your organization and the software vendor and/or a consulting firm. Together they will develop a detailed plan and deliverable dates for all phases of the project. This plan will be used to hold all parties accountable through each of the project phases.

Design and Build

The design and build phases are when your organization's business requirements are gathered and translated into how to configure your new system(s). As stated earlier, any HCM implementation is a tremendous opportunity for change. It is important to consider this when going into the process. A "lift and shift" mentality where you take what you have today and move it to the new platform should be avoided at all costs. Your team should have the mindset of redesigning systems and processes to work more efficiently. The focus should be on creating a more consumer-like experience around a modern cloud-based HR suite of products. A good vendor or consulting firm will help drive this change and introduce new concepts and processes, pushing your implementation team to think differently and drive change.

The *design phase* is where business requirements are gathered and documented. In this phase, Subject Matter Experts meet with Functional Product experts to document requirements. Typically, this process consists of a series of analysis meetings (virtual or in-person) led by Functional Product Experts. Each HCM vendor will operate the meetings based on their products and methodology, but the process generally consists of Functional Product Experts asking a series of targeted questions to get an understanding of how your HCM processes and procedures operate. The meetings are usually broken out into functional areas like taxes, payroll, direct access/self-service, performance, benefits, compensation, and succession. Subject Matter Experts from each HR area will attend these meetings to provide the specifics around each function. Prior to analysis meetings, your internal teams should be gathering documentation that outlines the processes today and those desired changes for the future. Some examples of items to gather are benefit plan summaries, payroll tax documentation, earning and deduction details, PTO plan summaries, payroll calendars, and performance review templates.

After the analysis is complete, you will likely receive a summary that outlines the design requirements. This typically comes in the form of a project scope document. The document is meant to confirm that the analysis accurately reflects the future state that your organization desires for HR operations. It is meant to guide the configuration of the new system and should be acknowledged and approved by your organization prior to building and configuration. This review and approval will ensure that your organization and the HCM vendor are aligned on requirements and will help to avoid any conflicts or confusion in the future.

At the conclusion of the design phase, you should have a clear understanding of the following:

- Configuration requirements including the organization structure, business rules, and user-defined fields
- Reporting requirements
- Integration points
- Gaps and the workarounds or custom development that may be available

The build phase is where the configuration of the application occurs, reports are created, and interfaces and conversion programs are developed. Any application customizations that have been identified and approved to be developed are performed in this phase. *Please note that depending on the vendor and software you are implementing, customs may or may not be permitted.*

The project manager from your organization will play a key role in coordinating resources in this phase and will need to work closely with your vendor project manager.

Each vendor will operate the build phase somewhat differently, but you can expect to be involved in some of the configuration of the system. This is a good opportunity to learn how the system functions and understand the process of maintenance. During the build phase, you will configure your company framework and business rules tables that set your system up to receive and maintain employee data. This will include everything from earnings and deductions, to job codes, to tracking company property.

In the cloud world, you may or may not have access to perform technical development. Your HCM vendor will work with you to identify the technical development team that will develop integrations and any customs that have been identified as part of the analysis. Integration building will require the collaboration of resources from your internal IT team and 3rd party vendor resources.

Report creation is another important task in the build phase. Most applications come with a standard set of reports, but any custom reports identified during analysis will be developed in the build phase. There will also be some work to align your existing set of reports to what is delivered by the vendor. This may happen during analysis but often comes as a second phase of design/build. Of all the areas in an implementation, reporting is often sacrificed when time or resources are not available. This leaves reporting as a "post-go-live" activity and can damage the perception of the implementation. It is important to keep this in mind and push to have all your reports ready and tested prior to going live.

The final and possibly the most critical piece of the build phase is data conversion. With this process, you will take all your existing data in legacy systems and convert it into the new system. The process will consist of a set of mapping exercises to ensure that your legacy codes for HR and payroll data will align with what you have configured in the new systems. A technical consultant will be assigned to walk you through this process. Once you have all the data mapped out correctly, you will export all the data from your legacy provider into a specific file format proved by the new vendor. The new data will then be parsed out and loaded into the system. This can be a complex process, so expect some bumps in the road and plan for multiple iterations to get the data loaded correctly.

Once the data is loaded, your team will be responsible for validating the information. You should be provided with a series of reports to assist with this process. Some vendors have advanced tools to facilitate the process as well. The key data points to look at during validation are below:

- Employee totals for active and terminated
- Accuracy of data on employee records (check for name suffixes, special characters, SSN, DOB)
- Job and Salary information
- Payroll balances and totals for YTD earnings, deductions, and taxes

Test

The Test Phase: This includes all the testing that is required to ensure the system has been implemented properly. There are functional tests designed to test that the processes are working as expected from a user perspective and technical tests that test that the processes are working from an application program perspective. If you are implementing a payroll system, there are a variety of tests that ensure your new payroll system is configured to calculate payroll accurately and tax employees appropriately.

For cloud-based HCM systems, most of the technical testing that you would see with an on-premise system is done behind the scenes by the vendor and is not something that your implementation team will have to get involved with. The only technical testing that your team is likely required to be involved in is on connection points for required integrations.

System Testing: Once your configuration is complete and employee records have been loaded into your new system, the System Consultant will run through a series of functional tests to ensure that the configurations are working properly. Depending on the product's set up, this could include a full cycle candidate application, running through workflow transactions, ensuring payroll processing steps work as expected, or a variety of other functions to ensure the programs are functioning properly. In most cases, your System Consultant will perform a system test to ensure that any issues identified are resolved prior to delivering the system to you and your team for user acceptance testing.

User Acceptance Testing: This is the phase where subject matter experts (SMEs) run tests against the application to make sure it meets stated requirements. While your project team may not have been involved in system testing, they will be heavily involved in User Acceptance Testing (UAT). Your team will test all systems to ensure they meet the requirements and are performing as expected. It is important to create test cases/scripts that outline the functions you are testing to compare expected results to the actual results of your testing. Vendors and implementation consultants will sometimes assist you with drafting test cases, but it is ultimately up to you as the client to create and manage UAT test cases. A simple excel grid with columns that outline the test case, who is performing the test, the date, the expected results, and the actual results are an excellent baseline for this effort. Having documented test cases with results will assist in tracking and resolving any issues that are flagged throughout the process.

The UAT process also provides valuable on-the-job training and ensures that you, as the client, understand the products and can sign off that systems are functioning as expected. By the end of UAT, most of your team will be familiar with the new technology, and your organization can sign off that the system is performing as expected from an end-user's perspective.

Payroll Parallel Testing: This is a functional test that ensures the payroll process in the current system is the same when the process is run in the new system. You can expect to be heavily involved in the parallel testing process. Users from your team will process test payrolls in the new system and ensure that results are as expected when compared with your existing payroll systems.

Typically, you will run through at least two rounds of parallel testing. During these tests, you will pick a check date from your existing payroll to compare the new payroll calculations against. You will import time data from that pay period into the new system along with any other earnings paid to employees on the applicable dates. You will then run the payroll through to the point where it is ready for validation. At that point, you will run reports from the new system to compare against how your legacy provider calculated the payroll. Some vendors will have tools to assist with this validation process, but most of the effort will revolve around generating reports from both systems to compare data. You will want to focus on making sure that the check totals balance in the two systems. You will look to ensure that all applicable earnings are paid, the right deductions are withheld, and that taxes are calculated accurately. Once you have identified and corrected any discrepancies from the first round of parallel testing, you will move onto the second round using a different check date.

When all testing is complete, you will most likely be asked to sign off that you approve the payroll process. This will be your final approval as you prepare for the go-live of the new system.

Go-Live

Go Live is the point in the project when you are ready to move to use your new system in a production environment. This is the point where all the hard work and dedication pays off, and that system you've been dreaming of becomes a reality. For a time and attendance and/or payroll implementation, it's the time when employees will start to clock in and out of the new system and when you will process your first payroll in the new system. For talent modules like applicant tracking, onboarding, or performance management tools, your go-live is the date you release the new products to internal and external customers for use.

The hard work of data conversion, testing and modifications are behind you at this point, but there are a few things to consider as you prepare for go-live.

Sunsetting Legacy Systems: Your new HR system will most often be replacing older systems. Before going live, you must ensure that all legacy vendors have been notified and access is adjusted for your internal and external customers. You will also want to ensure that all your integrations with legacy providers are deactivated and that vendors are prepared to receive information from your new system.

Preparation of the Production Environment: As you prepare for the launch of new systems, there are a variety of items that need to be addressed just before go-live. This could include a cleanup of final test data, scripts that need to be run to ready the system, and last-minute minor setting adjustments. Your vendor or System Consultant will most likely have a checklist of items to run through with you and your team to ensure you are fully prepared for go-live. Much of this work will be done behind the scenes by the vendor, but there may be some tasks that you have to complete, so it is something to be prepared for.

Support

After going live, there is a transition period where the implementation team will continue to provide support before turning over the application to the vendor support team.

During the transition, you will be introduced to your new support team through a series of calls. These calls will include introductions and a run-through of open items with your implementation team. Any outstanding items assigned to the implementation team will be documented, and your core team will most likely work through those issues until they are resolved.

Once you have been live on the new system(s) for a few weeks and open items have been resolved, the implementation team will phase out. All new support items will run through the support channels the vendor has in place.

CHAPTER 6: CHANGE MANAGEMENT

As previously mentioned, all system implementation projects come with a tremendous opportunity for change. Some change will be driven by differences in how a new vendor's technology functions vs. a legacy system. This type of change is unavoidable and will need to be managed. Change based on system differences should not be the only type of change you need to manage, however. It is important to investigate all your existing HR processes and find opportunities for change with any implementation. You should be asking if there are ways to do things differently, automate processes, implement direct access/self-service features, or make changes to how you work to better your HR operations.

It is human nature to be wary of change, but your organization will have champions of change as well. These individuals will embrace change and should be utilized as a part of the change management process as ambassadors and leaders of change. A well thought out change plan that has promoters of the change can be the difference between a successful implementation and what is perceived as a failure.

Best practice and HRchitect methodology uses a six phased approach to change management with HCM implementation projects. The six phases include Stakeholder Analysis, Impact Analysis, Ownership (RACI Identification), Communication Strategy, a Learning/Training Plan, and Go Live Readiness.

Stakeholder Identification and Impact Analysis

Stakeholder Identification and Impact Analysis are the processes of identifying the people that will be impacted by the change and the specific impacts on their daily routines and how they work. Stakeholders can include managers, employees, IT, HR Admins, leaders, vendors, and/or HR practitioners. They could be any user that will be either directly or indirectly using the HCM system.

Once you have identified the stakeholders, it is important to document how they will be impacted. There can be a wide variety and range of impacts on stakeholders. How are employees accessing paystubs? What is the process for a manager to change an employee's job or submit a salary increase for approval? How are vendor feeds being modified due to new systems being in place? Documenting all these changes is a key step to managing change.

Ownership

After stakeholders and impacts have been established, it is vital to establish a role and responsibility matrix for the execution of the change plan. This is done in the form of a RACI Chart.

You will need to identify people to act as Change Sponsors, Change Leaders, and Change Agents. The Change Sponsor sets the vision and expectations for the Change Team and has final approval authority for change activities. Change Leaders are leaders within their own organization that will support and drive the vision and monitor progress. Change Leaders serve as escalation points for Change Agents within their organization as well. Change Agents are "boots on the ground" resources that will enact the change plan. They will serve as points of contact for employees and managers as questions or concerns come about.

The RACI chart is a simple matrix used to assign the change roles and the responsibilities they will have for each impact that has been identified. Assigning a role to each impact will help keep change management initiatives moving. RACI assignments are defined as Responsible, Accountable, Consulted, and Informed. Definitions of each are shown below:

- **Responsible:** This team member does the work to complete the task. Every task needs at least one Responsible party, but it's okay to assign more.
- **Accountable:** This person delegates work and is the last one to review the task or deliverable before it's deemed complete. For some tasks, the Responsible party may also serve as the Accountable one. Just be sure you only have one Accountable person assigned to each task or deliverable.
- **Consulted:** Every deliverable is strengthened by review and consultation from more than one team member. Consulted parties are typically the people who provide input based on either how it will impact their future project work or their domain of expertise on the deliverable itself.
- **Informed:** These team members simply need to be kept in the loop on project progress rather than roped into the details of every

deliverable.

Below is a sample of a Change Management RACI Chart.

	R =	Responsible
SAMPLE **RACI**	A =	Accountable
	C =	Consulted
	I =	Informed

Task	Change Sponsor	Change Leader	Change Agent
Define vision for change	R		
Stakeholder identification	R	A	
Change impact analysis	R	A	
Determine obstacles and levers for change	R	A	C

Communication

It cannot be understated how critical Communication is to a change management initiative. Change management communication requires a strategy and a plan to execute. The communication strategy will determine the approach that will be followed when creating a communication plan. The following are some best practice communication principles to consider when strategizing your communication plan:

- Provide comprehensive and tailored communications that target specific audiences
- Communicate quickly, honestly, and often
- Manage people's expectations and deliver on promises
- Be clear, concise, and candid about the outcomes for the business, teams, and individuals

Using the principles of the strategy you define, you should create a targeted and specific communication plan based on the stages of your implementation project plan. The communication plan will be used to identify and track all types of communications, including targeted emails, mailers, posters/flyers, and intranet posts, for each of the stakeholder groups.

Your plan should define the following for each communication:

- Audience
- Purpose
- Format/Vehicle
- Date/Frequency
- Owners for Development and Delivery
- Status and Completion

Learning and Training

Following your communication plan, you will want to define a learning strategy to determine the approach that will be followed when creating a learning plan. Your learning/training plan will provide education to all system users about the process and system changes, so they can be comfortable with any process changes and new tools they will need to use.

Things to consider when defining your learning/training strategy:
- How do people in your organization learn?
- What tools do they need to be successful?
- How much time do they have for training?
- What technology can be leveraged?

Your learning plan will be used to identify and track all types of training to be delivered, including classroom, virtual, self-directed, and job aids, for each of the stakeholder groups. The plan should define for each activity:
- Audience
- Purpose
- Delivery Method
- Location (for in-person events)
- Date/Frequency
- Owners for Development and Delivery
- Status and Completion

There are three stages to think about when defining a learning plan. First, you want to define training topics, then group topics into courses/training programs, and finally assign the courses.

Training topics: Based on the need for training identified for each stakeholder, create the list of topics that need to be covered with training. Include the type of material available to be used for the creation of training content, and who will be responsible for the creation and delivery of the content.

Training courses: Group topics into courses. Some topics may be offered in multiple courses if they are applicable to multiple audiences. Define course length and delivery method (classroom, virtual, etc).

Course assignment: Assign stakeholders to any and all courses that they will be required to or requested to attend.

The final aspect to consider with learning/training is ensuring that you assign your courses at the appropriate time. You want to phase out learning so that stakeholders are taking training at the appropriate phase of the project. An example would be training payroll users on how to process payroll just before payroll testing or training HR Administrators on how to process employee changes just before dual maintenance starts. If you train too early, you run the risk of users forgetting what they learn. Train too late, and users will not be prepared for certain phases of the project.

Go-Live Readiness

The final component of managing change with an HCM implementation process is Go Live readiness. This requires creating a plan for ongoing adoption and support of the system and processes after the go-live. You will want to establish ownership of system and process documentation as a first step. The owners of the new system will be held accountable for the following:

- Serving as the "help desk" for end-user support
- Training for new users
- Creating a process for taking system change requests from users
- Monitoring system updates from the vendor

After going live, you will want to monitor the success of the implementation and change management efforts. We recommended that you survey your employee population to understand where you had success and where there are areas for improvement. Another way to gauge the success of change management efforts is through monitoring service desk tickets and calls. If you experience large spikes in certain areas, it's a good indication that change efforts missed the mark in that area. These measurement efforts will aid in future projects, system enhancements, and managing future change.

Change management should not be overlooked with your implementation efforts. Without change management, it will be difficult, if not impossible, to successfully roll out a new system and get adoption from users in your organization.

CHAPTER 7: LIVING WITH HCM SYSTEMS POST-IMPLEMENTATION

Resources

The resources required to support your application will come from your software vendor, internally within your organization, and optionally through consultants. Since the actual application is in the cloud, the vendor will be providing the technical support of the application, including applying upgrades, bug fixes, and hardware maintenance. Your internal team needs to be focused on the functional business needs and application configuration. You will need resources who understand how the application is configured, the data relationships, and how workflow and other processes work. Common job titles for these HR Roles contain HRIS/HRIT in the title.

The number of resources of the HRIS/HRIT team will, in part, be determined by the number of applications managed and the complexity of those applications. These resources may reside in HR or IT and, in rare instances, Finance or Operations. Some organizations will decide not to invest in employee resources and obtain support from third party consulting firms. Wherever the resources are housed, the primary role of these individuals is to support the users of the applications and maintain these applications for the organization.

Specific responsibilities include:

- **Application Configuration:** Post-implementation, there will be a need to make changes to the application, both as business needs change and as enhancements are delivered by the vendor. Trained Resources are needed to make these configurations. An organization may want to obtain a support contract from a consulting firm in lieu of having a team of trained application configurers.

- **Process Documentation:** Maintaining documentation on how processes are designed to work, the business reasons for the design, and the implications to other processes that are dependent upon them.

- **Data Quality and Management:** Setting data standards is key to ensure the applications are reliable and adopted. When data quality is compromised, the organization will begin creating its own information resources, and the HCM credibility and thus, usability will be compromised. While most of these elements will be established during implementation, updating them as business needs change is important.
  - Data definitions should include the valid values for the data.
  - Business rules should state how the data is to be used, if it is required or not, and the retention period (how long the data is to be kept).

- **Record Retention:** Record retention is the length of time a record is to be retained before being archived or deleted. This will be determined by legal and practical considerations. When records are no longer desired in your production system, they can be archived to another source if they are still needed for reference. If they are no longer needed for business operations or legally must be destroyed, they should be deleted from the application.

- **Enhancements/Upgrades/Fixes:** From time to time, the application vendor will make changes to the application. They could be in the form of enhancements or upgrades which provide additional features and functions or "Fixes" which correct an issue with how the application operates. The best practice is to have separate system environments to facilitate these changes as they are being made. In addition to your production environment, a test system should be in place to evaluate the impact the change has on your application. Once the vendor releases the new version of the software, you need to review the update and understand its impact on your existing processes and configurations. You also need to determine if new features should be implemented to improve your processes or user experience.

- **Business Continuity:** Business continuity refers to the plans and processes that will allow the business teams to operate in the event of a disaster. A plan needs to be in place for the unlikely event your HCM system is not available due to a disaster.

- **Data Privacy:** Information in the HCM system is personal and confidential. Great care must be taken to ensure that this information is kept private and not used for inappropriate means and that it is secure. Data privacy policies and practices must be established. As of this writing, the U.S. does not have any data privacy laws, but in most other countries, personal data is governed very closely. Having a knowledgeable attorney in each country the company operates is advised. If an organization does not have in-house attorneys, there are third party legal firms that will provide this service.

- **Security Management:** Management of security roles is an important responsibility. As people change jobs, and as the use of your HCM system evolves over time, new roles and information access will need to be established. Additionally, most organizations have audit requirements that need to be met. A solid security role management policy and process need to be enacted.

Processes

To maintain your HCM Applications, you will need to establish processes for approving and implementing changes to modules, workflow, and other configuration elements. You will also want to establish a formal review with your software vendor periodically and at contract renewal.

- **Change Request Process:** After implementation, business needs will change, and stakeholders will be requesting changes to the application. Some changes will be minor, others significant. Having a formal process to submit these is key. The process should include who can submit a request, whom the request is sent to, and who will approve the requests.

- **Prioritization of Changes:** Once changes have been approved, they need to be prioritized. This will ensure you are delivering the highest need/value add changes first, and thus increasing the return on investment (ROI) in the application. It is also helpful to establish a prioritization team made up of stakeholders from each area of the organization. The prioritization team, as a collective group, can discuss the merits of each request and gain consensus.

- **Testing Changes:** Some changes are minor and will not require significant testing, such as the adding of a job code. Other changes are more impactful, like the addition of a new time off plan, and require a more thorough test. Having test processes, including who will be responsible for creating the test plan and scenarios, who will execute the tests, and who will sign off that the testing has been successful, are critical so that new changes are deployed appropriately.

- **Deploying Changes:** The process of deployment of change is about when the change will be effective. When thinking about the effective date of the change, one must take into consideration the processes the change impacts. For example, if the change will impact a payroll result, you may want to deploy the change at the beginning of a pay period. The key is to deploy the change in time or when it is needed without impact on existing processes.

- **Report Requests:** As the adoption of the HCM applications grows, users will be asking for information from the system for decision making and other business purposes. While many applications have easy tools for people to use and create their own reports, best practice would have a centralized function responsible for this and "push" the data out either through email or on an application "dashboard." In this way, when decisions are made, the use of data is consistent, and there are not multiple versions of similar reports being used. Thus, a process for requesting and creating reports needs to be established.

- **Managing Vendor Support Requests:** There will be times when you request support from your vendor. These requests will include things that are not working as expected, the system not being available at all, and requests for assistance with implementing new functionality. Most software vendors will have an online application you can access to open and manage these requests, called "tickets." Alternatively, you may have a support contact that you can call directly. Either way, you will need a couple of individuals who are responsible for submitting these requests and managing them to resolution.

- **Application Review with Account Manager:** Periodically, but no less than twice per year, you will want to have a discussion with your Vendor Account Manager to make sure you are getting the most value from your investment. The topics of these meetings should be new features and functions, modules that you are not using, as well as any customer service issues that you have encountered.

CHAPTER 8: APPLYING YOUR HCM TECHNOLOGY KNOWLEDGE

Now that you've developed a strong foundation of HCM technology knowledge, what's next? You're ready to assess your organization's current state as it relates to HCM technology.

Start by asking yourself these questions:
- While reading this book, at any point did you think, "we don't even have a defined HR service delivery strategy or an HCM technology strategy"?
- Does your organization still have manual processes in place to support your organization's HR Service Delivery?
- If your organization has systems in place, are your existing systems outdated, riddled with issues requiring you to use workarounds, or generally a point of frustration for your HR team?
- Are you expecting the budget approval process to find a new system or replace an outdated system to be an uphill battle?
- Are you hesitant to take on an HCM technology-related project, even though your organization would benefit from this project because you're too busy with day-to-day responsibilities?

If you've answered "yes" to any of these questions, then you've got some work to do. Let's get to it!
1. Start by visiting www.HRchitect.com for more resources deep-diving into each subject area covered in the individual chapters.
2. Request a complimentary consultation with the HRchitect strategic services team by filling out the form here:

https://hrchitect.com/contact/. You can also send an email in to HCMtechnologybook@HRchitect.com. Our team will schedule a time to meet with you virtually to discuss your organization's specific HCM technology challenges. We'll offer practical tips and solutions to address those challenges.

3. Work with HRchitect! Our strategic services team is here to guide you through your HCM technology journey. Whether you need help defining your organization's HCM technology strategy in line with your service delivery model, building a business case to obtain board or executive approval of an HCM technology project, help facilitating the system evaluation or selection process, help implementing your new system, change management, ongoing system support, or anything in between, HRchitect is here to help.

ABOUT HRCHITECT

The world of Human Capital Management (HCM) is constantly changing. Are you prepared to start a new HCM technology initiative without an expert by your side?

HRchitect, the leading HCM technology consulting firm, offers you relief from this volatile situation by pairing your company with expert consultants who lead your team through your HCM technology challenges, whether that be creating a strategic plan for HCM technology, evaluating and selecting a new or replacement system, system implementation, project management, change management, system optimization, or ongoing support.

HRchitect is the only consulting firm that focuses solely on HCM technology and delivers expertise around the full lifecycle of HCM technology from Core HR, Benefits, Payroll, Talent Acquisition, Talent Management, Workforce Management, and everything in between. Since 1997, HRchitect has helped thousands of organizations worldwide of all sizes and industries get more from their HCM technology.

For more information, or to connect with the HRchitect team for a complimentary HCM technology consultation, please visit HRchitect's website.

ABOUT THE AUTHORS

Jacqueline Kuhn

Jacqueline Kuhn is an HR professional with over 25 years' experience in Strategic Planning, Systems Management, Project Management, HR Service Delivery, and General Human Resources. Throughout Jacqueline's career, she has worked with organizations in all sectors, global and domestic, to create strategic plans around their Human Capital Management systems, as well as leading selection and implementation projects for all types of HCM technology.

In her role at HRchitect, she oversees the strategic consulting group, which encompasses HRchitect's HCM systems strategic planning, evaluation and selection, and change management practices. Jacqueline spends much of her time with HCM vendors being briefed on their technology offerings, ensuring that HRchitect provides the most current information to our clients looking for new solutions. Jacqueline enjoys working with organizations to impact their HCM strategies through the utilization of technology.

Jacqueline is a Certified Professional of Human Resource Information (HRIP). She is a highly sought-after speaker at industry events. Her work has been published in professional magazines and journals. When she isn't working with HRchitect clients, Jacqueline enjoys dog training and is also a classically trained Pianist.

Julia Hatton

Julia Hatton is a Senior Strategic Services Consultant at HRchitect. Julia brings over 20 years of combined consulting and HR practitioner experience to the HRchitect team. Having led HCM technology system evaluations and implementations for many years as an HR practitioner, the transition to consulting was a natural evolution for Julia. In her current role, she focuses on guiding clients through HRchitect's strategic planning and system evaluation & selection processes, helping them address challenges, understanding where they want to be with HCM technology, and recommending options for how to best get there.

When she is not working with HRchitect clients, Julia enjoys spending time with her four-legged children (2 rescue dogs), pursuing her love of photography, and volunteering at an animal rescue and food bank in her local community.

Andrew Schweihs

Andrew Schweihs has over 10 years of professional Human Resources experience. His strategic HR consulting experience includes system selection, vision workshops, HCM technology recommendations and roadmaps, and change management initiatives. Prior to joining HRchitect, he started his consulting career leading full-lifecycle HRIS and payroll system implementations including both system design and technical implementation components.

Dixie Vaughan

Dixie Vaughan has over 30 years of experience with HCM systems, with particular expertise specific to HRIS system design and implementation. Before her retirement in 2020, Dixie was a Senior Consultant at HRchitect, where she helped organizations create HCM technology strategies, evaluate and select systems, and implement systems. Prior to joining HRchitect, she worked as an HR technologist across various industries, including healthcare, non-profit, technology, and hospitality. She is currently enjoying her retirement traveling with her husband.

Made in the USA
Middletown, DE
06 October 2023